WINE, WATER AND SONG

and

POEMS

Two Volumes

by
G. K. CHESTERTON

NATAL PUBLISHING LLC
ARS LONGA, VITA BREVIS

Copyright© 2024 Natal Publishing

All rights reserved

Cover art by Mauricio A. on Pixabay

CONTENTS
(Wine, Water and Song)

The Englishman

Wine and Water

The Song against Grocers

The Rolling English Road

The Song of Quoodle

Pioneers, O Pioneers

The Logical Vegetarian

"The Saracen's Head"

The Good Rich Man

The Song against Songs

Me Heart

The Song of the Oak

The Road to Roundabout

The Song of the Strange Ascetic

The Song of Right and Wrong

Who Goes Home?

CONTENTS
(Poems)

I

THREE DEDICATIONS

TO EDMUND CLERIHEW BENTLEY
TO HILAIRE BELLOC
TO M. E. W.

II

WAR POEMS

LEPANTO
THE MARCH OF THE BLACK MOUNTAIN 1913
BLESSED ARE THE PEACEMAKERS
THE WIFE OF FLANDERS
THE CRUSADER RETURNS FROM CAPTIVITY

III

LOVE POEMS

GLENCOE
LOVE'S TRAPPIST
CONFESSIONAL
MUSIC
THE DELUGE
THE STRANGE MUSIC
THE GREAT MINIMUM
THE MORTAL ANSWERS
A MARRIAGE SONG
BAY COMBE

IV

RELIGIOUS POEMS

THE WISE MEN
THE HOUSE OF CHRISTMAS
A SONG OF GIFTS TO GOD
THE KINGDOM OF HEAVEN
A HYMN FOR THE CHURCH MILITANT

THE BEATIFIC VISION
THE TRUCE OF CHRISTMAS
A HYMN
A CHRISTMAS SONG FOR THREE GUILDS
THE NATIVITY
A CHILD OF THE SNOWS
A WORD

V

RHYMES FOR THE TIMES

ANTICHRIST, OR THE REUNION OF CHRISTENDOM: AN ODE
THE REVOLUTIONIST, OR LINES TO A STATESMAN
THE SHAKESPEARE MEMORIAL
THE HORRIBLE HISTORY OF JONES
THE NEW FREETHINKER
IN MEMORIAM P.D.
SONNET WITH THE COMPLIMENTS OF THE SEASON
A SONG OF SWORDS
A SONG OF DEFEAT
SONNET
AFRICA
THE DEAD HERO
AN ELECTION ECHO 1906
THE SONG OF THE WHEELS
THE SECRET PEOPLE

VI

MISCELLANEOUS POEMS

LOST
BALLAD OF THE SUN
TRANSLATION FROM DU BELLAY
THE HIGHER UNITY
THE EARTH'S VIGIL
ON RIGHTEOUS INDIGNATION
WHEN I CAME BACK TO FLEET STREET
A CIDER SONG
THE LAST HERO

VII

BALLADES

BALLADE D'UNE GRANDE DAME
A BALLADE OF AN ANTI-PURITAN
A BALLADE OF A BOOK-REVIEWER
A BALLADE OF SUICIDE
A BALLADE OF THE FIRST RAIN

The Englishman

ST. GEORGE he was for England,
And before he killed the dragon
He drank a pint of English ale
Out of an English flagon.
For though he fast right readily
In hair-shirt or in mail,
It isn't safe to give him cakes
Unless you give him ale.

St. George he was for England,
And right gallantly set free
The lady left for dragon's meat
And tied up to a tree;
But since he stood for England
And knew what England means,
Unless you give him bacon
You mustn't give him beans.

St. George he is for England,
And shall wear the shield he wore
When we go out in armour
With the battle-cross before.
But though he is jolly company
And very pleased to dine,
It isn't safe to give him nuts
Unless you give him wine.

Wine and Water

OLD Noah he had an ostrich farm and fowls on the largest scale,
He ate his egg with a ladle in an egg-cup big as a pail,
And the soup he took was Elephant Soup and the fish he took was
    Whale,
But they all were small to the cellar he took when he set out to sail,
And Noah he often said to his wife when he sat down to dine,
"I don't care where the water goes if it doesn't get into the wine."

The cataract of the cliff of heaven fell blinding off the brink
As if it would wash the stars away as suds go down a sink,
The seven heavens came roaring down for the throats of hell to drink,

And Noah he cocked his eye and said, "It looks like rain, I think,
The water has drowned the Matterhorn as deep as a Mendip mine,
But I don't care where the water goes if it doesn't get into the wine."

But Noah he sinned, and we have sinned; on tipsy feet we trod,
Till a great big black teetotaller was sent to us for a rod,
And you can't get wine at a P.S.A., or chapel, or Eisteddfod,
For the Curse of Water has come again because of the wrath of God,
And water is on the Bishop's board and the Higher Thinker's shrine,
But I don't care where the water goes if it doesn't get into the wine.

The Song Against Grocers

GOD made the wicked Grocer
For a mystery and a sign,
That men might shun the awful shops
And go to inns to dine;
Where the bacon's on the rafter
And the wine is in the wood,
And God that made good laughter
Has seen that they are good.

The evil-hearted Grocer
Would call his mother "Ma'am,"
And bow at her and bob at her,
Her aged soul to damn,
And rub his horrid hands and ask
What article was next,
Though ***mortis in articulo***
Should be her proper text.

His props are not his children,
But pert lads underpaid,
Who call out "Cash!" and bang about
To work his wicked trade;
He keeps a lady in a cage
Most cruelly all day,
And makes her count and calls her "Miss"
Until she fades away.

The righteous minds of innkeepers
Induce them now and then
To crack a bottle with a friend

Or treat unmoneyed men,
But who hath seen the Grocer
Treat housemaids to his teas
Or crack a bottle of fish-sauce
Or stand a man a cheese?

He sells us sands of Araby
As sugar for cash down;
He sweeps his shop and sells the dust
The purest salt in town,
He crams with cans of poisoned meat
Poor subjects of the King,
And when they die by thousands
Why, he laughs like anything.

The wicked Grocer groces
In spirits and in wine,
Not frankly and in fellowship
As men in inns do dine;
But packed with soap and sardines
And carried off by grooms,
For to be snatched by Duchesses
And drunk in dressing-rooms.

The hell-instructed Grocer
Has a temple made of tin,
And the ruin of good innkeepers
Is loudly urged therein;
But now the sands are running out
From sugar of a sort,
The Grocer trembles; for his time,
Just like his weight, is short.

The Rolling English Road

BEFORE the Roman came to Rye or out to Severn strode,
The rolling English drunkard made the rolling English road.
A reeling road, a rolling road, that rambles round the shire,
And after him the parson ran, the sexton and the squire;
A merry road, a mazy road, and such as we did tread
The night we went to Birmingham by way of Beachy Head.

I knew no harm of Bonaparte and plenty of the Squire,

And for to fight the Frenchman I did not much desire;
But I did bash their baggonets because they came arrayed
To straighten out the crooked road an English drunkard made,
Where you and I went down the lane with ale-mugs in our hands,
The night we went to Glastonbury by way of Goodwin Sands.

His sins they were forgiven him; or why do flowers run
Behind him; and the hedges all strengthing in the sun?
The wild thing went from left to right and knew not which was
    which,
But the wild rose was above him when they found him in the ditch.
God pardon us, nor harden us; we did not see so clear
The night we went to Bannockburn by way of Brighton Pier.

My friends, we will not go again or ape an ancient rage,
Or stretch the folly of our youth to be the shame of age,
But walk with clearer eyes and ears this path that wandereth,
And see undrugged in evening light the decent inn of death;
For there is good news yet to hear and fine things to be seen,
Before we go to Paradise by way of Kensal Green.

The Song of Quoodle

THEY haven't got no noses,
The fallen sons of Eve;
Even the smell of roses
Is not what they supposes;
But more than mind discloses
And more than men believe.

They haven't got no noses,
They cannot even tell
When door and darkness closes
The park a Jew encloses,
Where even the Law of Moses
Will let you steal a smell.

The brilliant smell of water,
The brave smell of a stone,
The smell of dew and thunder,
The old bones buried under,
Are things in which they blunder
And err, if left alone.

The wind from winter forests,
The scent of scentless flowers,
The breath of brides' adorning,
The smell of snare and warning,
The smell of Sunday morning,
God gave to us for ours.

. . . . .

And Quoodle here discloses
All things that Quoodle can,
They haven't got no noses,
They haven't got no noses,
And goodness only knowses
The Noselessness of Man.

Pioneers, O Pioneers

NEBUCHADNEZZAR the King of the Jews
Suffered from new and original views,
He crawled on his hands and knees, it's said,
With grass in his mouth and a crown on his head.
With a wowtyiddly, etc.

Those in traditional paths that trod
Thought the thing was a curse from God,
But a Pioneer men always abuse
Like Nebuchadnezzar the King of the Jews.

Black Lord Foulon the Frenchman slew
Thought it a Futurist thing to do.
He offered them grass instead of bread.
So they stuffed him with grass when they cut off his head.
With a wowtyiddly, etc.

For the pride of his soul he perished then—
But of course it is always of Pride that men,
A Man in Advance of his Age accuse,
Like Nebuchadnezzar the King of the Jews.

Simeon Scudder of Styx, in Maine,
Thought of the thing and was at it again.
He gave good grass and water in pails
To a thousand Irishmen hammering rails.

With a wowtyiddly, etc.

Appetites differ; and tied to a stake
He was tarred and feathered for Conscience' Sake.
But stoning the prophets is ancient news,
Like Nebuchadnezzar the King of the Jews.

The Logical Vegetarian

"Why shouldn't I have a purely vegetarian drink? Why shouldn't I take vegetables in their highest form, so to speak? The modest vegetarians ought obviously to stick to wine or beer, plain vegetarian drinks, instead of filling their goblets with the blood of bulls and elephants, as all conventional meat-eaters do, I suppose."—DALROY.

YOU will find me drinking rum,
Like a sailor in a slum,
You will find me drinking beer like a Bavarian.
You will find me drinking gin
In the lowest kind of inn,
Because I am a rigid Vegetarian.

So I cleared the inn of wine,
And I tried to climb the sign,
And I tried to hail the constable as "Marion."
But he said I couldn't speak,
And he bowled me to the Beak
Because I was a Happy Vegetarian.

Oh, I knew a Doctor Gluck,
And his nose it had a hook,
And his attitudes were anything but Aryan;
So I gave him all the pork
That I had, upon a fork;
Because I am myself a Vegetarian.

I am silent in the Club,
I am silent in the pub.,
I am silent on a bally peak in Darien;
For I stuff away for life
Shoving peas in with a knife,
Because I am at heart a Vegetarian.

No more the milk of cows

Shall pollute my private house
Than the milk of the wild mares of the Barbarian;
I will stick to port and sherry,
For they are so very, very,
So very, very, very Vegetarian.

"The Saracen's Head"

"THE Saracen's Head" looks down the lane,
Where we shall never drink wine again,
For the wicked old women who feel well-bred
Have turned to a tea-shop "The Saracen's Head."

"The Saracen's Head" out of Araby came,
King Richard riding in arms like flame,
And where he established his folk to be fed
He set up a spear—and the Saracen's Head.

But "The Saracen's Head" outlived the Kings,
It thought and it thought of most horrible things,
Of Health and of Soap and of Standard Bread,
And of Saracen drinks at "The Saracen's Head."

So "The Saracen's Head" fulfils its name,
They drink no wine—a ridiculous game—
And I shall wonder until I'm dead,
How it ever came into the Saracen's Head.

The Good Rich Man

MR. MANDRAGON, the Millionaire, he wouldn't have wine or
    wife,
He couldn't endure complexity: he lived the Simple Life.
He ordered his lunch by megaphone in manly, simple tones,
And used all his motors for canvassing voters, and twenty telephones;
Besides a dandy little machine,
Cunning and neat as ever was seen,
With a hundred pulleys and cranks between,
Made of metal and kept quite clean,
To hoist him out of his healthful bed on every day of his life,

And wash him and dress him and shave him and brush him
—to live the Simple Life.

Mr. Mandragon was most refined and quietly, neatly dressed,
Say all the American newspapers that know refinement best;
Quiet and neat the hat and hair and the coat quiet and neat,
A trouser worn upon either leg, while boots adorn the feet;
And not, as any one would expect,
A Tiger's Skin all striped and specked,
And a Peacock Hat with the tail erect,
A scarlet tunic with sunflowers decked,
Which might have had a more marked effect,
And pleased the pride of a weaker man that yearned for wine or wife;
But Fame and the Flagon, for Mr. Mandragon
—obscured the Simple Life.

Mr. Mandragon, the Millionaire, I am happy to say, is dead;
He enjoyed a quiet funeral in a Crematorium shed.
And he lies there fluffy and soft and grey and certainly quite refined;
When he might have rotted to flowers and fruit with Adam and all
    mankind,
Or been eaten by wolves athirst for blood,
Or burnt on a good tall pyre of wood,
In a towering flame, as a heathen should,
Or even sat with us here at food,
Merrily taking twopenny ale and pork with a pocket-knife;
But this was luxury not for one that went for the Simple Life.

The Song Against Songs

THE song of the sorrow of Melisande is a weary song and a dreary
    song,
The glory of Mariana's grange had got into great decay,
The song of the Raven Never More has never been called a cheery
    song,
And the brightest things in Baudelaire are anything else but gay.

But who will write us a riding song,
Or a hunting song or a drinking song,
Fit for them that arose and rode
When day and the wine were red?
But bring me a quart of claret out,
And I will write you a clinking song,

A song of war and a song of wine
And a song to wake the dead.

The song of the fury of Fragolette is a florid song and a torrid song,
The song of the sorrow of Tara is sung to a harp unstrung,
The song of the cheerful Shropshire Lad I consider a perfectly horrid
    song,
And the song of the happy Futurist is a song that can't be sung.

But who will write us a riding song
Or a fighting song or a drinking song,
Fit for the fathers of you and me,
That knew how to think and thrive?
But the song of Beauty and Art and Love
Is simply an utterly stinking song,
To double you up and drag you down
And damn your soul alive.

Me Heart

I COME from Castlepatrick, and me heart is on me sleeve,
And any sword or pistol boy can hit it with me leave,
It shines there for an epaulette, as golden as a flame,
As naked as me ancestors, as noble as me name.
For I come from Castlepatrick, and me heart is on me sleeve,
But a lady stole it from me on St. Gallowglass's Eve.

The folk that live in Liverpool, their heart is in their boots;
They go to hell like lambs, they do, because the hooter hoots.
Where men may not be dancin', though the wheels may dance all
    day;
And men may not be smokin'; but only chimneys may.
But I come from Castlepatrick, and me heart is on me sleeve,
But a lady stole it from me on St. Poleander's Eve.

The folk that live in black Belfast, their heart is in their mouth,
They see us making murders in the meadows of the South;
They think a plough's a rack, they do, and cattle-calls are creeds,
And they think we're burnin' witches when we're only burnin'
    weeds;
But I come from Castlepatrick, and me heart is on me sleeve;
But a lady stole it from me on St. Barnabas's Eve.

The Song of the Oak

THE Druids waved their golden knives
And danced around the Oak
When they had sacrificed a man;
But though the learned search and scan,
No single modern person can
Entirely see the joke.
But though they cut the throats of men
They cut not down the tree,
And from the blood the saplings sprang
Of oak-woods yet to be.
But Ivywood, Lord Ivywood,
He rots the tree as ivy would,
He clings and crawls as ivy would
About the sacred tree.

King Charles he fled from Worcester fight
And hid him in an Oak;
In convent schools no man of tact
Would trace and praise his every act,
Or argue that he was in fact
A strict and sainted bloke,
But not by him the sacred woods
Have lost their fancies free,
And though he was extremely big
He did not break the tree.
But Ivywood, Lord Ivywood,
He breaks the tree as ivy would,
And eats the woods as ivy would
Between us and the sea.

Great Collingwood walked down the glade
And flung the acorns free,
That oaks might still be in the grove
As oaken as the beams above,
When the great Lover sailors love
Was kissed by Death at sea.
But though for him the oak-trees fell
To build the oaken ships,
The woodman worshipped what he smote
And honoured even the chips.
But Ivywood, Lord Ivywood,
He hates the tree as ivy would,
As the dragon of the ivy would
That has us in his grips.

Wine, Water and Song

The Road to Roundabout

SOME say that Guy of Warwick,
The man that killed the Cow
And brake the mighty Boar alive
Beyond the Bridge at Slough;
Went up against a Loathly Worm
That wasted all the Downs,
And so the roads they twist and squirm
(If I may be allowed the term)
From the writhing of the stricken Worm
That died in seven towns.
I see no scientific proof
That this idea is sound,
And I should say they wound about
To find the town of Roundabout,
The merry town of Roundabout,
That makes the world go round.

Some say that Robin Goodfellow,
Whose lantern lights the meads
(To steal a phrase Sir Walter Scott
In heaven no longer needs),
Such dance around the trysting-place
The moonstruck lover leads;
Which superstition I should scout
There is more faith in honest doubt
(As Tennyson has pointed out)
Than in those nasty creeds.
But peace and righteousness (St. John)
In Roundabout can kiss,
And since that's all that's found about
The pleasant town of Roundabout,
The roads they simply bound about
To find out where it is.

Some say that when Sir Lancelot
Went forth to find the Grail,
Grey Merlin wrinkled up the roads
For hope that he should fail;
All roads led back to Lyonesse
And Camelot in the Vale,
I cannot yield assent to this
Extravagant hypothesis,
The plain, shrewd Briton will dismiss

Such rumours (*Daily Mail*).
But in the streets of Roundabout
Are no such factions found,
Or theories to expound about,
Or roll upon the ground about,
In the happy town of Roundabout,
That makes the world go round.

The Song of the Strange Ascetic

IF I had been a Heathen,
I'd have praised the purple vine,
My slaves should dig the vineyards,
And I would drink the wine;
But Higgins is a Heathen,
And his slaves grow lean and grey,
That he may drink some tepid milk
Exactly twice a day.

If I had been a Heathen,
I'd have crowned Neœra's curls,
And filled my life with love affairs,
My house with dancing girls;
But Higgins is a Heathen,
And to lecture rooms is forced,
Where his aunts, who are not married,
Demand to be divorced.

If I had been a Heathen,
I'd have sent my armies forth,
And dragged behind my chariots
The Chieftains of the North.
But Higgins is a Heathen,
And he drives the dreary quill,
To lend the poor that funny cash
That makes them poorer still.

If I had been a Heathen,
I'd have piled my pyre on high,
And in a great red whirlwind
Gone roaring to the sky;
But Higgins is a Heathen,
And a richer man than I;

And they put him in an oven,
Just as if he were a pie.

Now who that runs can read it,
The riddle that I write,
Of why this poor old sinner,
Should sin without delight—?
But I, I cannot read it
(Although I run and run),
Of them that do not have the faith,
And will not have the fun.

The Song of Right and Wrong

FEAST on wine or fast on water,
And your honour shall stand sure,
God Almighty's son and daughter
He the valiant, she the pure;
If an angel out of heaven
Brings you other things to drink,
Thank him for his kind attentions,
Go and pour them down the sink.

Tea is like the East he grows in,
A great yellow Mandarin
With urbanity of manner
And unconsciousness of sin;
All the women, like a harem,
At his pig-tail troop along;
And, like all the East he grows in,
He is Poison when he's strong.

Tea, although an Oriental,
Is a gentleman at least;
Cocoa is a cad and coward,
Cocoa is a vulgar beast,
Cocoa is a dull, disloyal,
Lying, crawling cad and clown,
And may very well be grateful
To the fool that takes him down.

As for all the windy waters,
They were rained like tempests down

When good drink had been dishonoured
By the tipplers of the town;
When red wine had brought red ruin
And the death-dance of our times,
Heaven sent us Soda Water
As a torment for our crimes.

Who Goes Home?

IN the city set upon slime and loam
They cry in their parliament "Who goes home?"
And there comes no answer in arch or dome,
For none in the city of graves goes home.
Yet these shall perish and understand,
For God has pity on this great land.

Men that are men again; who goes home?
Tocsin and trumpeter! Who goes home?
For there's blood on the field and blood on the foam
And blood on the body when Man goes home.
And a voice valedictory.... Who is for Victory?
Who is for Liberty? Who goes home?

POEMS
by
G.K. CHESTERTON

I

THREE DEDICATIONS

TO EDMUND CLERIHEW BENTLEY

THE DEDICATION OF *THE MAN WHO WAS THURSDAY*

A cloud was on the mind of men, and wailing went the weather,
Yea, a sick cloud upon the soul when we were boys together.
Science announced nonentity and art admired decay;
The world was old and ended: but you and I were gay.
Round us in antic order their crippled vices came—
Lust that had lost its laughter, fear that had lost its shame.
Like the white lock of Whistler, that lit our aimless gloom,
Men showed their own white feather as proudly as a plume.
Life was a fly that faded, and death a drone that stung;
The world was very old indeed when you and I were young.
They twisted even decent sin to shapes not to be named:
Men were ashamed of honour; but we were not ashamed.
Weak if we were and foolish, not thus we failed, not thus;
When that black Baal blocked the heavens he had no hymns from us.
Children we were—our forts of sand were even as weak as we,
High as they went we piled them up to break that bitter sea.
Fools as we were in motley, all jangling and absurd,
When all church bells were silent our cap and bells were heard.

Not all unhelped we held the fort, our tiny flags unfurled;
Some giants laboured in that cloud to lift it from the world.
I find again the book we found, I feel the hour that flings
Far out of fish-shaped Paumanok some cry of cleaner things;
And the Green Carnation withered, as in forest fires that pass,
Roared in the wind of all the world ten million leaves of grass;
Or sane and sweet and sudden as a bird sings in the rain
Truth out of Tusitala spoke and pleasure out of pain.
Yea, cool and clear and sudden as a bird sings in the grey,
Dunedin to Samoa spoke, and darkness unto day,
But we were young; we lived to see God break their bitter charms,

God and the good Republic come riding back in arms:
We have seen the city of Mansoul, even as it rocked, relieved—Blessed
are they who did not see, but being blind, believed.

This is a tale of those old fears, even of those emptied hells,
And none but you shall understand the true thing that it tells—
Of what colossal gods of shame could cow men and yet crash,
Of what huge devils hid the stars, yet fell at a pistol flash.
The doubts that were so plain to chase, so dreadful to withstand—
Oh, who shall understand but you; yea, who shall understand?
The doubts that drove us through the night as we two talked amain,
And day had broken on the streets e'er it broke upon the brain.
Between us, by the peace of God, such truth can now be told;
Yea, there is strength in striking root, and good in growing old.
We have found common things at last, and marriage and a creed.
And I may safely write it now, and you may safely read.

TO HILAIRE BELLOC

THE DEDICATION OF *THE NAPOLEON OF NOTTING HILL*

For every tiny town or place
God made the stars especially;
Babies look up with owlish face
And see them tangled in a tree:
You saw a moon from Sussex Downs,
A Sussex moon, untravelled still,
I saw a moon that was the town's,
The largest lamp on Campden Hill.

Yea, Heaven is everywhere at home.
The big blue cap that always fits,
And so it is (be calm; they come
To goal at last, my wandering wits),
So it is with the heroic thing;
This shall not end for the world's end,
And though the sullen engines swing,
Be you not much afraid, my friend.

This did not end by Nelson's urn
Where an immortal England sits—
Nor where your tall young men in turn
Drank death like wine at Austerlitz.

And when the pedants bade us mark
What cold mechanic happenings
Must come; our souls said in the dark,
"Belike; but there are likelier things."

Likelier across these flats afar,
These sulky levels smooth and free,
The drums shall crash a waltz of war
And Death shall dance with Liberty;
Likelier the barricades shall blare
Slaughter below and smoke above,
And death and hate and hell declare
That men have found a thing to love.

Far from your sunny uplands set
I saw the dream; the streets I trod,
The lit straight streets shot out and met
The starry streets that point to God;
The legend of an epic hour
A child I dreamed, and dream it still,
Under the great grey water-tower
That strikes the stars on Campden Hill

TO *M. E. W.*

Words, for alas my trade is words, a barren burst of rhyme,
Rubbed by a hundred rhymesters, battered a thousand times,
Take them, you, that smile on strings, those nobler sounds than mine,
The words that never lie, or brag, or flatter, or malign.

I give a hand to my lady, another to my friend,
To whom you too have given a hand; and so before the end
We four may pray, for all the years, whatever suns beset,
The sole two prayers worth praying—to live and not forget.

The pale leaf falls in pallor, but the green leaf turns to gold;
We that have found it good to be young shall find it good to be old;
Life that bringeth the marriage bell, the cradle and the grave,
Life that is mean to the mean of heart, and only brave to the brave.

In the calm of the last white winter, when all the past is ours,
Old tears are frozen as jewels, old storms frosted as flowers.
Dear Lady, may we meet again, stand up again, we four,
Beneath the burden of the years, and praise the earth once more.

II

WAR POEMS

LEPANTO

White founts falling in the Courts of the sun,
And the Soldan of Byzantium is smiling as they run;
There is laughter like the fountains in that face of all men feared,
It stirs the forest darkness, the darkness of his beard,
It curls the blood-red crescent, the crescent of his lips,
For the inmost sea of all the earth is shake with his ships.
They have dared the white republics up the cape of Italy,
They have dashed the Adriatic round the Lion of the Sea,
And the Pope has cast his arms abroad for agony and loss,
And called the kings of Christendom for swords about the Cross.
The cold queen of England is looking in the glass;
The shadow of the Valois is yawning at the Mass;
From evening isles fantastical rings faint the Spanish gun,
And the Lord upon the Golden Horn is laughing in the sun.

Dim drums throbbing, in the hills half heard,
Where only on a nameless throne a crownless prince has stirred,
Where, risen from a doubtful seat and half attainted stall,
The last knight of Europe takes weapons from the wall,
The last and lingering troubadour to whom the bird has sung,
That once went singing southward when all the world was young.
In that enormous silence, tiny and unafraid,
Comes up along a winding road the noise of the Crusade.

Strong gongs groaning as the guns boom far,
Don John of Austria is going to the war,
Stiff flags straining in the night-blasts cold
In the gloom black-purple, in the glint old-gold,
Torchlight crimson on the copper kettle-drums,
Then the tuckets, then the trumpets, then the cannon, and he comes.
Don John laughing in the brave beard curled.
Spuming of his stirrups like the thrones of all the world,
Holding his head up for a flag of all the free.
Love-light of Spain—hurrah!
Death-light of Africa!
Don John of Austria
Is riding to the sea.

Mahound is in his paradise above the evening star,
(Don John of Austria is going to the war.)
He moves a mighty turban on the timeless houri's knees,
His turban that is woven of the sunsets and the seas.
He shakes the peacock gardens as he rises from his ease,
And he strides among the tree-tops and is taller than the trees,
And his voice through all the garden is a thunder sent to bring
Black Azrael and Ariel and Ammon on the wing.
Giants and the Genii,
Multiplex of wing and eye,
Whose strong obedience broke the sky
When Solomon was king.

They rush in red and purple from the red clouds of the morn,
From temples where the yellow gods shut up their eyes in scorn;
They rise in green robes roaring from the green hells of the sea
Where fallen skies and evil hues and eyeless creatures be;
On them the sea-valves cluster and the grey sea-forests curl,
Splashed with a splendid sickness, the sickness of the pearl;
They swell in sapphire smoke out of the blue cracks of the ground,—
They gather and they wonder and give worship to Mahound.
And he saith, "Break up the mountains where the hermit-folk can hide,
And sift the red and silver sands lest bone of saint abide,
And chase the Giaours flying night and day, not giving rest,
For that which was our trouble comes again out of the west.
We have set the seal of Solomon on all things under sun,
Of knowledge and of sorrow and endurance of things done,
But a noise is in 'the mountains, in the mountains, and I know
The voice that shook our palaces—four hundred years ago:
It is he that saith not 'Kismet'; it is he that knows not Fate;
It is Richard, it is Raymond, it is Godfrey in the gate!
It is he whose loss is laughter when he counts the wager worth,
Put down your feet upon him, that our peace be on the earth."
For he heard drums groaning and he heard guns jar,
(Don John of Austria is going to the war.)
Sudden and still—hurrah!
Bolt from Iberia!
Don John of Austria
Is gone by Alcalar.

St. Michael's on his Mountain in the sea-roads of the north
(Don John of Austria is girt and going forth.)
Where the grey seas glitter and the sharp tides shift
And the sea-folk labour and the red sails lift.

He shakes his lance of iron and he claps his wings of stone;
The noise is gone through Normandy; the noise is gone alone;
The North is full of tangled things and texts and aching eyes
And dead is all the innocence of anger and surprise,
And Christian killeth Christian in a narrow dusty
And Christian dreadeth Christ that hath a newer face of doom,
And Christian hateth Mary that God kissed in Galilee,
But Don John of Austria is riding to the sea.
Don John calling through the blast and the eclipse
Crying with the trumpet, with the trumpet of his lips,
Trumpet that sayeth ha!
Domino gloria!
Don John of Austria
Is shouting to the ships.

King Philip's in his closet with the Fleece about his neck
(Don John of Austria is armed upon the deck.)
The walls are hung with velvet that is black and soft as sin,
And little dwarfs creep out of it and little dwarfs creep in.
He holds a crystal phial that has colours like the moon,
He touches, and it tingles, and he trembles very
And his face is as a fungus of a leprous white and grey
Like plants in the high houses that are shuttered from the day.
And death is in the phial and the end of noble work,
But Don John of Austria has fired upon the Turk.
Don John's hunting, and his hounds have bayed—Booms
away past Italy the rumour of his raid.
Gun upon gun, ha! ha!
Gun upon gun, hurrah!
Don John of Austria
Has loosed the cannonade.

The Pope was in his chapel before day or battle broke,
(Don John of Austria is hidden in the smoke.)
The hidden room in man's house where God sits all the year,
The secret window whence the world looks small and very dear.
He sees as in a mirror on the monstrous twilight sea
The crescent of his cruel ships whose name is mystery;
They fling great shadows foe-wards, making Cross and Castle dark,
They veil the plumed lions on the galleys of St. Mark;
And above the ships are palaces of brown, black-bearded chiefs,
And below the ships are prisons, where with multitudinous griefs,
Christian captives sick and sunless, all a labouring race repines
Like a race in sunken cities, like a nation in the mines.
They are lost like slaves that swat, and in the skies of morning hung

The stair-ways of the tallest gods when tyranny was young.
They are countless, voiceless, hopeless as those fallen or fleeing on
Before the high Kings' horses in the granite of Babylon.
And many a one grows witless in his quiet room in hell
Where a yellow face looks inward through the lattice of his cell,
And he finds his God forgotten, and he seeks no more a sign *(But
Don John of Austria has burst the battle-line!)*
Don John pounding from the slaughter-painted poop,
Purpling all the ocean like a bloody pirate's sloop,
Scarlet running over on the silvers and the golds,
Breaking of the hatches up and bursting of the holds,
Thronging of the thousands up that labour under sex
White for bliss and blind for sun and stunned for liberty.
Vivat Hispania!
Domino Gloria!
Don John of Austria
Has set his people free!

Cervantes on his galley sets the sword back in the sheath
(Don John of Austria rides homeward with a wreath.)
And he sees across a weary land a straggling road in Spain,
Up which a lean and foolish knight for ever rides in vain,
And he smiles, but not as Sultans smile, and settles back the blade....
(But Don John of Austria rides home from the Crusade.)

THE MARCH OF THE BLACK MOUNTAIN 1913

What will there be to remember
Of us in the days to be?
Whose faith was a trodden ember
And even our doubt not free;
Parliaments built of paper,
And the soft swords of gold
That twist like a waxen taper
In the weak aggressor's hold;
A hush around Hunger, slaying
A city of serfs unfed;
What shall we leave for a saying
To praise us when we are dead?
But men shall remember the Mountain
That broke its forest chains,
And men shall remember the Mountain
When it arches against the plains:
And christen their children from it

And season and ship and street,
When the Mountain came to Mahomet
And looked small before his feet.

His head was as high as the crescent
Of the moon that seemed his crown,
And on glory of past and present
The light of his eyes looked down;
One hand went out to the morning
Over Brahmin and Buddhist slain,
And one to the West in scorning
To point at the scars of Spain;
One foot on the hills for warden
By the little Mountain trod;
And one was in a garden
And stood on the grave of God.
But men shall remember the Mountain,
Though it fall down like a tree,
They shall see the sign of the Mountain
Faith cast into the sea;
Though the crooked swords overcome it
And the Crooked Moon ride free,
When the Mountain comes to Mahomet
It has more life than he.

But what will there be to remember
Or what will there be to see—
Though our towns through a long November
Abide to the end and be?
Strength of slave and mechanic
Whose iron is ruled by gold,
Peace of immortal panic,
Love that is hate grown cold—
Are these a bribe or a warning
That we turn not to the sun,
Nor look on the lands of morning
Where deeds at last are done?
Where men shall remember the Mountain
When truth forgets the plain—
And walk in the way of the Mountain
That did not fail in vain;
Death and eclipse and comet,
Thunder and seals that rend:
When the Mountain came to Mahomet;
Because it was the end.

BLESSED ARE THE PEACEMAKERS

Of old with a divided heart
I saw my people's pride expand,
Since a man's soul is torn apart
By mother earth and fatherland.

I knew, through many a tangled tale,
Glory and truth not one but two:
King, Constable, and Amirail
Took me like trumpets: but I knew

A blacker thing than blood's own dye
Weighed down great Hawkins on the sea;
And Nelson turned his blindest eye
On Naples and on liberty.

Therefore to you my thanks, O throne,
O thousandfold and frozen folk,
For whose cold frenzies all your own
The Battle of the Rivers broke;

Who have no faith a man could mourn.
Nor freedom any man desires;
But in a new clean light of scorn
Close up my quarrel with my sires;

Who bring my English heart to me,
Who mend me like a broken toy;
Till I can see you fight and flee,
And laugh as if I were a boy.

THE WIFE OF FLANDERS

Low and brown barns thatched and repatched and tattered
Where I had seven sons until to-day,
A little hill of hay your spur has scattered....
This is not Paris. You have lost the way.

You, staring at your sword to find it brittle,
Surprised at the surprise that was your plan,
Who shaking and breaking barriers not a little
Find never more the death-door of Sedan.

Must I for more than carnage call you claimant,
Paying you a penny for each son you slay?
Man, the whole globe in gold were no repayment
For what *you* have lost. And how shall I repay?

What is the price of that red spark that caught me
From a kind farm that never had a name?
What is the price of that dead man they brought me?
For other dead men do not look the same.

How should I pay for one poor graven steeple
Whereon you shattered what you shall not know,
How should I pay you, miserable people?
How should I pay you everything you owe?34

Unhappy, can I give you back your honour?
Though I forgave would any man forget?
While all the great green land has trampled on her
The treason and terror of the night we met.

Not any more in vengeance or in pardon
An old wife bargains for a bean that's hers.
You have no word to break: no heart to harden.
Ride on and prosper. You have lost your spurs.

THE CRUSADER RETURNS FROM CAPTIVITY

I have come forth alive from the land of purple and poison and glamour,
Where the charm is strong as the torture, being chosen to change the mind;
Torture of wordless dance and wineless feast without clamour,
Palace hidden in palace, garden with garden behind;

Women veiled in the sun, or bare as brass in the shadows,
And the endless eyeless patterns where each thing seems an eye....
And my stride is on Caesar's sand where it slides to the English meadows,
To the last low woods of Sussex and the road that goes to Rye.

In the cool and careless woods the eyes of the eunuchs burned not,
But the wild hawk went before me, being free to return or roam,

The hills had broad unconscious backs; and the tree-tops turned not,
And the huts were heedless of me: and I knew I was at home.

And I saw my lady afar and her holy freedom upon her,
A head, without veil, averted, and not to be turned with charms,
And I heard above bannerets blown the intolerant trumpets of honour,
That usher with iron laughter the coming of Christian arms.

My shield hangs stainless still; but I shall not go where they praise it,
A sword is still at my side, but I shall not ride with the King.
Only to walk and to walk and to stun my soul and amaze it,
A day with the stone and the sparrow and every marvellous thing.

I have trod the curves of the Crescent, in the maze of them that adore it,
Curved around doorless chambers and unbeholden abodes,
But I walk in the maze no more; on the sign of the cross I swore it,
The wild white cross of freedom, the sign of the white cross-roads.

And the land shall leave me or take, and the Woman take me or leave me,
There shall be no more Night, or nightmares seen in a glass;
But Life shall hold me alive, and Death shall never deceive me
As long as I walk in England in the lanes that let me pass.

III

LOVE POEMS

GLENCOE

The star-crowned cliffs seem hinged upon the sky,
The clouds are floating rags across them curled,
They open to us like the gates of God
Cloven in the last great wall of all the world.

I looked, and saw the valley of my soul
Where naked crests fight to achieve the skies,
Where no grain grows nor wine, no fruitful thing,

Only big words and starry blasphemies.

But you have clothed with mercy like a moss
The barren violence of its primal wars,
Sterile although they be and void of rule,
You know my shapeless crags have Wed the stars.

How shall I thank you, O courageous heart.
That of this wasteful world you had no fear;
But bade it blossom in clear faith and sent
Your fair flower-feeding rivers: even as here

The peat burns brimming from their cups of stone
Glow brown and blood-red down the vast decline
As if Christ stood on yonder clouded peak
And turned its thousand waters into wine.

LOVE'S TRAPPIST

There is a place where lute and lyre are broken.
Where scrolls are torn and on a wild wind go,
Where tablets stand wiped naked for a token,
Where laurels wither and the daisies grow.

Lo: I too join the brotherhood of silence,
I am Love's Trappist and you ask in vain,
For man through Love's gate, even as through Death's gate,
Goeth alone and comes not back again.

Yet here I pause, look back across the threshold.
Cry to my brethren, though the world be old,
Prophets and sages, questioners and doubters,
O world, old world, the best hath ne'er been told!

CONFESSIONAL

Now that I kneel at the throne, O Queen,
Pity and pardon me.
Much have I striven to sing the same,
Brother of beast and tree;
Yet when the stars catch me alone

Never a linnet sings—
And the blood of a man is a bitter voice
And cries for foolish things.

Not for me be the vaunt of woe;
Was not I from a boy
Vowed with the helmet and spear and spur
To the blood-red banner of joy?
A man may sing his psalms to a stone,
Pour his blood for a weed,
But the tears of a man are a sudden thing,
And come not of his creed.

Nay, but the earth is kind to me,
Though I cry for a Star,
Leaves and grasses, feather and flower,
Cover the foolish scar,
Prophets and saints and seraphim
Lighten the load with song,
And the heart of a man is a heavy load
For a man to bear along.

MUSIC

Sounding brass and tinkling cymbal,
He that made me sealed my ears,
And the pomp of gorgeous noises,
Waves of triumph, waves of tears,

Thundered empty round and past me,
Shattered, lost for ever more,
Ancient gold of pride and passion,
Wrecked like treasure on a shore.

But I saw her cheek and forehead
Change, as at a spoken word,
And I saw her head uplifted
Like a lily to the Lord.

Nought is lost, but all transmuted,
Ears are sealed, yet eyes have seen;
Saw her smiles (O soul be worthy!),
Saw her tears (O heart be clean!).

THE DELUGE

Though giant rains put out the sun,
Here stand I for a sign.
Though Earth be filled with waters dark,
My cup is filled with wine.
Tell to the trembling priests that here
Under the deluge rod,
One nameless, tattered, broken man
Stood up and drank to God.

Sun has been where the rain is now,
Bees in the heat to hum,
Haply a humming maiden came,
Now let the Deluge come:
Brown of aureole, green of garb,
Straight as a golden rod,
Drink to the throne of thunder now!
Drink to the wrath of God.

High in the wreck I held the cup,
I clutched my rusty sword,
I cocked my tattered feather
To the glory of the Lord.
Not undone were the heaven and earth,
This hollow world thrown up,
Before one man had stood up straight!
And drained it like a cup.

THE STRANGE MUSIC

Other loves may sink and settle, other loves may loose and slack,
But I wander like a minstrel with a harp upon his back,
Though the harp be on my bosom, though I finger and I fret,
Still, my hope is all before me: for I cannot play it yet.

In your strings is hid a music that no hand hath ere let fall,
In your soul is sealed a pleasure that you have not known at all;
Pleasure subtle as your spirit, strange and slender as your frame,
Fiercer than the pain that folds you, softer than your sorrow's name.

Not as mine, my soul's anointed, not as mine the rude and light

Easy mirth of many faces, swaggering pride of song and fight;
Something stranger, something sweeter, something waiting you afar,
Secret as your stricken senses, magic as your sorrows are.

But on this, God's harp supernal, stretched but to be stricken once.
Hoary Time is a beginner, Life a bungler, Death a dunce.
But I will not fear to match them—no, by God, I will not fear,
I will learn you, I will play you and the stars stand still to hear.

THE GREAT MINIMUM

It is something to have wept as we have wept,
It is something to have done as we have done,
It is something to have watched when all men slept,
And seen the stars which never see the sun.

It is something to have smelt the mystic rose,
Although it break and leave the thorny rods,
It is something to have hungered once as those
Must hunger who have ate the bread of gods.

To have seen you and your unforgotten face,
Brave as a blast of trumpets for the fray.
Pure as white lilies in a watery space,
It were something, though you went from me to-day.

To have known the things that from the weak are furled,
Perilous ancient passions, strange and high;
It is something to be wiser than the world,
It is something to be older than the sky.

In a time of sceptic moths and cynic rusts,
And fatted lives that of their sweetness tire,
In a world of flying loves and fading lusts,
It is something to be sure of a desire.

Lo, blessed are our ears for they have heard;
Yea, blessed are our eyes for they have seen:
Let thunder break on man and beast and bird
And the lightning. It is something to have been.

THE MORTAL ANSWERS

..................COME AWAY—
WITH THE FAIRIES, HAND IN HAND,
FOR THE WORLD IS MORE FULL OF WEEPING
THAN YOU CAN UNDERSTAND.

W.B. Yeats.

From the Wood of the Old Wives' Fables
They glittered out of the grey,
And with all the Armies of Elf-land
I strove like a beast at bay;

With only a right arm wearied,
Only a red sword worn,
And the pride of the House of Adam
That holdeth the stars in scorn.

For they came with chains of flowers
And lilies lances free,
There in the quiet greenwood
To take my grief from me.

And I said, "Now all is shaken
When heavily hangs the brow,
When the hope of the years is taken
The last star sunken. Now—

"Hear, you chattering cricket,
Hear, you spawn of the sod,
The strange strong cry in the darkness
Of one man praising God,

"That out of the night and nothing
With travail of birth he came
To stand one hour in the sunlight
Only to say her name.

"Falls through her hair the sunshine
In showers; it touches, see,
Her high bright cheeks in turning;
Ah, Elfin Company,

"The world is hot and cruel,
We are weary of heart and hand.
But the world is more full of glory
Than you can understand."

A MARRIAGE SONG

Why should we reck of hours that rend
While we two ride together?
The heavens rent from end to end
Would be but windy weather,
The strong stars shaken down in spate
Would be a shower of spring,
And we should list the trump of fate
And hear a linnet sing.

We break the line with stroke and luck,
The arrows run like rain,
If you be struck, or I be struck,
There's one to strike again.
If you befriend, or I befriend,
The strength is in us twain,
And good things end and bad things end,
And you and I remain.

Why should we reck of ill or well
While we two ride together?
The fires that over Sodom fell
Would be but sultry weather.
Beyond all ends to all men given
Our race is far and fell,
We shall but wash our feet in heaven,
And warm our hands in hell.

Battles unborn and vast shall view
Our faltered standards stream,
New friends shall come and frenzies new.
New troubles toil and teem;
New friends shall pass and still renew
One truth that does not seem,
That I am I, and you are you,
And Death a morning dream.

Why should we reck of scorn or praise
While we two ride together?
The icy air of godless days
Shall be but wintry weather.
If hell were highest, if the heaven
Were blue with devils blue,
I should have guessed that all was even,
If I had dreamed of you.

Little I reck of empty prides,
Of creeds more cold than clay;
To nobler ends and longer rides,
My lady rides to-day.
To swing our swords and take our sides
In that all-ending fray
When stars fall down and darkness hides,
When God shall turn to bay.

Why should we reck of grin and groan
While we two ride together?
The triple thunders of the throne
Would be but stormy weather.
For us the last great fight shall roar,
Upon the ultimate plains,
And we shall turn and tell once more
Our love in English lanes.

BAY COMBE

With leaves below and leaves above,
And groping under tree and tree,
I found the home of my true love,
Who is a wandering home for me.

Who, lost in ruined worlds aloof,
Bore the dread dove wings like a roof;
Who, past the last lost stars of space
Carried the fire-light on her face.

Who, passing as in idle hours,
Tamed the wild weeds to garden flowers;
Stroked the strange whirlwind's whirring wings,
And made the comets homely things.

Where she went by upon her way
The dark was dearer than the day;
Where she paused in heaven or hell,
The whole world's tale had ended well.

With leaves below and leaves above.
And groping under tree and tree,
I found the home of my true love,
Who is a wandering home for me.

Where she was flung, above, beneath,
By the rude dance of life and death,
Grow she at Gotham—die at Rome,
Between the pine trees is her home.

In some strange town, some silver morn,
She may have wandered to be born;
Stopped at some motley crowd impressed,
And called them kinsfolk for a jest.

If we again En goodness thrive,
And the dead saints become alive,
Then pedants bald and parchments brown
May claim her blood for London town.

But leaves below and leaves above.
And groping under tree and tree,
I found the home of my true love,
Who is a wandering home for me.

The great gravestone she may pass by,
And without noticing, may die;
The streets of silver Heaven may tread,
With her grey awful eyes unfed.

The city of great peace in pain
May pass, until she find again
This little house of holm and fir
God built before the stars for her.

Here in the fallen leaves is furled
Her secret centre of the world.
We sit and feel in dusk and dun
The stars swing round us like a sun.

For leaves below and leaves above.
And groping under tree and tree,
I found the home of my true love.
Who is a wandering home for me.

IV

RELIGIOUS POEMS

THE WISE MEN

Step softly, under snow or rain,
To find the place where men can pray;
The way is all so very plain
That we may lose the way.

Oh, we have learnt to peer and pore
On tortured puzzles from our youth,
We know all labyrinthine lore,
We are the three wise mert of yore,
And we know all things but the truth.

We have gone round and round the hill,
And lost the wood among the trees,
And learnt long names for every ill,
And served the mad gods, naming still
The Furies the Eumenides.

The gods of violence took the veil
Of vision and philosophy,
The Serpent that brought all men bale,
He bites his own accursed tail,
And calls himself Eternity.

Go humbly ... it has hailed and snowed ...
With voices low and lanterns lit;
So very simple is the road,
That we may stray from it.

The world grows terrible and white,
And blinding white the breaking day;

We walk bewildered in the light,
For something is too large for sight,
And something much too plain to say.

The Child that was ere worlds begun
(... We need but walk a little way,
We need but see a latch undone,...)
The Child that played with moon and sun
Is playing with a little hay.

The house from which the heavens are fed,
The old strange house that is our own,
Where tricks of words are never said.
And Mercy is as plain as bread,
And Honour is as hard as stone.

Go humbly; humble are the skies,
And low and large and fierce the Star;
So very near the Manger lies
That we may travel far.

Hark! Laughter like a lion wakes
To roar to the resounding plain,
And the whole heaven shouts and shakes,
For God Himself is born again,
And we are little children walking
Through the snow and rain.

THE HOUSE OF CHRISTMAS

There fared a mother driven forth
Out of an inn to roam;
In the place where she was homeless
All men are at home.
The crazy stable close at hand,
With shaking timber and shifting sand,
Grew a stronger thing to abide and stand
Than the square stones of Rome.

For men are homesick in their homes,
And strangers under the sun,
And they lay their heads in a foreign land
Whenever the day is done.

Here we have battle and blazing eyes,
And chance and honour and high surprise,
Where the yule tale was begun.

A Child in a foul stable,
Where the beasts feed and foam;
Only where He was homeless
Are you and I at home;
We have hands that fashion and heads that
But our hearts we lost—how long ago!
In a place no chart nor ship can show
Under the sky's dome.

This world is wild as an old wives' tale,
And strange the plain things are,
The earth is enough and the air is enough
For our wonder and our war;
But our rest is as far as the fire-drake swings
And our peace is put in impossible things
Where clashed and thundered unthinkable wings
Round an incredible star.

To an open house in the evening
Home shall men come,
To an older place than Eden
And a taller town than Rome.
To the end of the way of the wandering star,
To the things that cannot be and that are,
To the place where God was homeless
And all men are at home.

A SONG OF GIFTS TO GOD

When the first Christmas presents came, the straw where Christ was rolled
Smelt sweeter than their frankincense, burnt brighter than their gold,
And a wise man said, "We will not give; the thanks would be but cold."

"Nay," said the next, "To all new gifts, to this gift or another,
Bends the high gratitude of God; even as He now, my brother,
Who had a Father for all time, yet thanks Him for a Mother.

"Yet scarce for Him this yellow stone or prickly-smells and sparse.

Who holds the gold heart of the sun that fed these timber bars,
Nor any scentless lily lives for One that smells the stars."

Then spake the third of the Wise Men; the wisest of the three:
"We may not with the widest lives enlarge His liberty,
Whose wings are wider than the world. It is not He, but we.

"We say not He has more to gain, but we have more to lose.
Less gold shall go astray, we say, less gold, if thus we choose,
Go to make harlots of the Greeks and hucksters of the Jews.

"Less clouds before colossal feet redden in the under-light,
To the blind gods from Babylon less incense burn to-night,
To the high beasts of Babylon, whose mouths make mock of right."

Babe of the thousand birthdays, we that are young yet grey,
White with the centuries, still can find no better thing to say,
We that with sects and whims and wars have wasted Christmas Day.

Light Thou Thy censer to Thyself, for all our fires are dim,
Stamp Thou Thine image on our coin, for Caesar's face grows dim,
And a dumb devil of pride and greed has taken hold of him.

We bring Thee back great Christendom, churches and towns and towers.
And if our hands are glad, O God, to cast them down like flowers,
'Tis not that they enrich Thine hands, but they are saved from ours.

THE KINGDOM OF HEAVEN

Said the Lord God, "Build a house,
Build it in the gorge of death,
Found it in the throats of hell.
Where the lost sea muttereth,
Fires and whirlwinds, build it well."

Laboured sternly flame and wind,
But a little, and they cry,
"Lord, we doubt of this Thy will,
We are blind and murmur why,"
And the winds are murmuring still.

Said the Lord God, "Build a house,

Cleave its treasure from the earth,
With the jarring powers of hell
Strive with formless might and mirth,
Tribes and war-men, build it well."

Then the raw red sons of men
Brake the soil, and lopped the wood,
But a little and they shrill,
"Lord, we cannot view Thy good,"
And the wild men clamour still.

Said the Lord God, "Build a house,
Smoke and iron, spark and steam,
Speak and vote and buy and sell;
Let a new world throb and stream,
Seers and makers, build it well."

Strove the cunning men and strong,
But a little and they cry,
"Lord, mayhap we are but clay,
And we cannot know the why,"
And the wise men doubt to-day.

Yet though worn and deaf and blind,
Force and savage, king and seer
Labour still, they know not why;
At the dim foundation here,
Knead and plough and think and ply.

Till at last, mayhap, hereon,
Fused of passion and accord,
Love its crown and peace its stay
Rise the city of the Lord
That we darkly build to-day.

A HYMN FOR THE CHURCH MILITANT

Great God, that bowest sky and star,
Bow down our towering thoughts to thee,
And grant us in a faltering war
The firm feet of humility.

Lord, we that snatch the swords of flame,

Lord, we that cry about Thy car.
We too are weak with pride and shame,
We too are as our foemen are.

Yea, we are mad as they are mad,
Yea, we are blind as they are blind,
Yea, we are very sick and sad
Who bring good news to all mankind.

The dreadful joy Thy Son has sent
Is heavier than any care;
We find, as Cain his punishment,
Our pardon more than we can bear.

Lord, when we cry Thee far and near
And thunder through all lands unknown
The gospel into every ear,
Lord, let us not forget our own.

Cleanse us from ire of creed or class,
The anger of the idle tings;
Sow in our souls, like living grass,
The laughter of all lowly things.

THE BEATIFIC VISION

Then Bernard smiled at me, that I should gaze
But I had gazed already; caught the view,
Faced the unfathomable ray of rays
Which to itself and by itself is true.

Then was my vision mightier than man's speech;
Speech snapt before it like a flying spell;
And memory and all that time can teach
Before that splendid outrage failed and fell.

As when one dreameth and remembereth not
Waking, what were his pleasures or his pains,
With every feature of the dream forgot,
The printed passion of the dream remains:—

Even such am I; within whose thoughts resides
No picture of that sight nor any part

Nor any memory: in whom abides
Only a happiness within the heart,

A secret happiness that soaks the heart
As hills are soaked by slow unsealing snow,
Or secret as that wind without a chart
Whereon did the wild leaves of Sibyl go.

O light uplifted from all mortal knowing,
Send back a little of that glimpse of thee.
That of its glory I may kindle glowing
One tiny spark for all men yet to be.

THE TRUCE OF CHRISTMAS

Passionate peace is in the sky—
And in the snow in silver sealed
The beasts are perfect in the field,
And men seem men so suddenly—
(But take ten swords and ten times ten
And blow the bugle in praising men;
For we are for all men under the sun,
And they are against us every one;
And misers haggle and madmen clutch,
And there is peril in praising much.
And we have the terrible tongues uncurled
That praise the world to the sons of the world.)

The idle humble hill and wood
Are bowed upon the sacred birth,
And for one little hour the earth
Is lazy with the love of good—
(But ready are you, and ready am I,
If the battle blow and the guns go by;
For we are for all men under the sun,
And they are against us every one;
And the men that hate herd all together,
To pride and gold, and the great white feather
And the thing is graven in star and stone
That the men who love are all alone.)

Hunger is hard and time is tough,
But bless the beggars and kiss the kings,

For hope has broken the heart of things,
And nothing was ever praised enough.
(But bold the shield for a sudden swing
And point the sword when you praise a thing,
For we are for all men under the sun,
And they are against us every one;
And mime and merchant, thane and thrall
Hate us because we love them all;
Only till Christmastide go by
Passionate peace is in the sky.)

A HYMN

O God of earth and altar,
Bow down and hear our cry
Our earthly rulers falter,
Our people drift and die;
The walls of gold entomb us,
The swords of scorn divide,
Take not thy thunder from us,
But take away our pride.

From all that terror teaches,
From lies of tongue and pen,
From all the easy speeches
That comfort cruel men,
From sale and profanation
Of honour and the sword,
From sleep and from damnation,
Deliver us, good Lord!

Tie in a living tether
The prince and priest and thrall,
Bind all our lives together,
Smite us and save us all;
In ire and exultation
Aflame with faith, and free,
Lift up a living nation,
A single sword to thee.

Poems

A CHRISTMAS SONG FOR THREE GUILDS

TO BE SUNG A LONG TIME AGO—OR HENCE

THE CARPENTERS

St. Joseph to the Carpenters said on a Christmas Day:
"The master shall have patience and the prentice shall obey;
And your word unto your women shall be nowise hard or wild:
For the sake of me, your master, who have worshipped Wife and Child.
But softly you shall frame the fence, and softly carve the door,
And softly plane the table—as to spread it for the poor,
And all your thoughts be soft and white as the wood of the white tree.
But if they tear the Charter, let the tocsin speak for me!
Let the wooden sign above your shop be prouder to be scarred
Than the lion-shield of Lancelot that hung at Joyous Garde."

THE SHOEMAKERS

St. Crispin to the shoemakers said on a Christmastide:
"Who fashions at another's feet will get no good of pride.
They were bleeding on the Mountain, the feet that brought good news,
The latchet of whose shoes we were not worthy to unloose.
See that your feet offend not, nor lightly lift your head,
Tread softly on the sunlit roads the bright dust of the dead.
Let your own feet be shod with peace; be lowly all your lives.
But if they touch the Charter, ye shall nail it with your knives.
And the bill-blades of the commons drive in all as dense array
As once a crash of arrows came, upon St. Crispin's Day."

THE PAINTERS

St. Luke unto the painters on Christmas Day he said:
"See that the robes are white you dare to dip in gold and red;
For only gold the kings can give, and only blood the saints;
And his high task grows perilous that mixes them in paints.
Keep you the ancient order; follow the men that knew
The labyrinth of black and whits, the maze of green and blue;
Paint mighty things, paint paltry things, paint silly things or sweet.
But if men break the Charter, you may slay them in the street.
And if you paint one post for them, then ... but you know it well,
You paint a harlot's face to drag all heroes down to hell."

ALL TOGETHER

Almighty God to all mankind on Christmas Day said He:
"I rent you from the old red hills and, rending, made you free.
There was charter, there was challenge; in a blast of breath I gave;
You can be all things other; you cannot be a slave.
You shall be tired and tolerant of fancies as they fade,
But if men doubt the Charter, ye shall call on the Crusade—
Trumpet and torch and catapult, cannon and bow and blade,
Because it was My challenge to all the things I made."

THE NATIVITY

The thatch on the roof was as golden,
Though dusty the straw was and old,
The wind had a peal as of trumpets,
Though blowing and barren and cold,
The mother's hair was a glory
Though loosened and torn,
For under the eaves in the gloaming
A child was born.

Have a myriad children been quickened.
Have a myriad children grown old,
Grown gross and unloved and embittered,
Grown cunning and savage and cold?
God abides In a terrible patience,
Unangered, unworn,
And again for the child that was squandered
A child is born.

What know we of æons behind us,
Dim dynasties lost long ago,
Huge empires, like dreams unremembered,
Huge cities for ages laid low?
This at least—that with blight and with blessing
With flower and with thorn,
Love was there, and his cry was among them,
"A child is born."

Though the darkness be noisy with systems,
Dark fancies that fret and disprove,
Still the plumes stir around us, above us

The wings of the shadow of love:
Oh! princes and priests, have ye seen it
Grow pale through your scorn.
Huge dawns sleep before us, deep changes,
A child is born.

And the rafters of toil still are gilded
With the dawn of the star of the heart,
And the wise men draw near in the twilight,
Who are weary of learning and art,
And the face of the tyrant is darkened.
His spirit is torn,
For a new King is enthroned; yea, the sternest,
A child is born.

And the mother still joys for the whispered
First stir of unspeakable things,
Still feels that high moment unfurling
Red glory of Gabriel's wings.
Still the babe of an hour is a master
Whom angels adorn,
Emmanuel, prophet, anointed,
A child is born.

And thou, that art still in thy cradle,
The sun being crown for thy brow.
Make answer, our flesh, make an answer,
Say, whence art thou come—who art thou?
Art thou come back on earth for our teaching
To train or to warn—?
Hush—how may we know?—knowing only
A child is born.

A CHILD OF THE SNOWS

There is heard a hymn when the panes dim
And never before or again,
When the nights are strong with a darkness long,
And the dark is alive with rain.

Never we know but in sleet and in snow,
The place where the great fires are,
That the midst of the earth is a raging mirth

And the heart of the earth a star.

And at night we win to the ancient inn
Where the child in the frost is furled,
We follow the feet where all souls meet
At the inn at the end of the world.

The gods lie dead where the leaves lie red,
For the flame of the sun is flown.
The gods lie cold where the leaves lie gold.
And a Child comes forth alone.

A WORD

A word came forth in Galilee, a word like to a star;
It climbed and rang and blessed and burnt wherever brave hearts are;
A word of sudden secret hope, of trial and increase
Of wrath and pity fused in fire, and passion kissing peace.
A star that o'er the citied world beckoned, a sword of flame;
A star with myriad thunders tongued: a mighty word there came.

The wedge's dart passed into it, the groan of timberwains,
The ringing of the rivet nails, the shrieking of the planes;
The hammering on the roofs at morn, the busy workshop roar;
The hiss of shavings drifted deep along the windy floor;
The heat-browned toiler's crooning song, the hum of human worth—
Mingled of all the noise of crafts, the ringing word went forth.

The splash of nets passed into it, the grind of sand and shell,
The boat-hook's clash, the boat-oars' jar, the cries to buy and sell,
The flapping of the landed shoals, the canvas crackling free,
And through all varied notes and cries, the roaring of the sea,
The noise of little lives and brave, of needy lives and high;
In gathering all the throes of earth, the living word went by.

Earth's giant sins bowed down to it, in Empire's huge eclipse,
When darkness sat above the thrones, seven thunders on her lips,
The woe of cities entered it, the clang of idols' falls,
The scream of filthy Caesars stabbed high in their brazen halls,
The dim hoarse floods of naked men, the worldrealms snapping girth,
The trumpets of Apocalypse, the darkness of the earth:

The wrath that brake the eternal lamp and hid the eternal hill,

A world's destruction loading, the word went onward still—
The blaze of creeds passed into it, the hiss of horrid fires,
The headlong spear, the scarlet cross, the hair-shirt and the briars,
The cloistered brethren's thunderous chaunt, the errant champion's song,
The shifting of the crowns and thrones, the tangle of the strong.

The shattering fall of crest and crown and shield and cross and cope,
The tearing of the gauds of time, the blight of prince and pope,
The reign of ragged millions leagued to wrench a loaded debt,
Loud with the many throated roar, the word went forward yet.
The song of wheels passed into it, the roaring and the smoke
The riddle of the want and wage, the fogs that burn and choke.
The breaking of the girths of gold, the needs that creep and swell.
The strengthening hope, the dazing light, the deafening evangel,
Through kingdoms dead and empires damned, through changes without cease,
With earthquake, chaos, born and fed, rose,—and the word was "Peace."

V

RHYMES FOR THE TIMES

ANTICHRIST, OR THE REUNION OF CHRISTENDOM: AN ODE

"A BILL WHICH HAS SHOCKED THE CONSCIENCE OF
EVERY CHRISTIAN COMMUNITY IN EUROPE."—
Mr. F.E. Smith, ON THE WELSH DISESTABLISHMENT BILL.

Are they clinging to their crosses,
F.E. Smith,
Where the Breton boat-fleet tosses,
Are they, Smith?
Do they, fasting, tramping, bleeding,
Wait the news from this our city?
Groaning "That's the Second Reading!"
Hissing "There is still Committed"
If the voice of Cecil falters,
If McKenna's point has pith,
Do they tremble for their altars?

Do they, Smith?

Russian peasants round their pope
Huddled, Smith,
Hear about it all, I hope,
Don't they, Smith?
In the mountain hamlets clothing
Peaks beyond Caucasian pales,
Where Establishment means nothing
And they never heard of Wales,
Do they read it all in Hansard
With a crib to read it with—
"Welsh Tithes: Dr. Clifford Answered,"
Really, Smith?

In the lands where Christians were,
F.E. Smith,
In the little lands laid bare,
Smith, O Smith!
Where the Turkish bands are busy,
And the Tory name is blessed
Since they hailed the Cross of Dizzy
On the banners from the West!
Men don't think it half so hard if
Islam burns their kin and kith,
Since a curate lives in Cardiff
Saved by Smith.

It would greatly, I must own,
Soothe me, Smith,
If you left this theme alone,
Holy Smith!
For your legal cause or civil
You fight well and get your fee;
For your God or dream or devil
You will answer, not to me.
Talk about the pews and steeples
And the Cash that goes therewith!
But the souls of Christian peoples....
—Chuck it, Smith!

Poems

THE REVOLUTIONIST: OR LINES TO A STATESMAN

"I WAS NEVER STANDING BY WHILE A REVOLUTION
WAS GOING ON."—*Speech by the Rt. Hon. Walter Long.*

When Death was on thy drums, Democracy,
And with one rush of slaves the world was free,
In that high dawn that Kings shall not forget,
A void there was and Walter was not yet.
Through sacked Versailles, at Valmy in the fray,
They did without him in some kind of way;
Red Christendom all Walterless they cross,
And in their fury hardly feel their loss....
Fades the Republic; faint as Roland's horn,
Her trumpets taunt us with a sacred scorn....
Then silence fell; and Mr. Long was born.

From his first hours in his expensive cot
He never saw the tiniest viscount shot.
In deference to his wealthy parents' whim
The wildest massacres were kept from him.
The wars that dyed Pall Mall and Brompton red
Passed harmless o'er that one unconscious head:
For all that little Long could understand
The rich might still be rulers of the land.
Vain are the pious arts of parenthood,
Foiled Revolution bubbled in his blood;
Until one day (the babe unborn shall rue it)
The Constitution bored him and he slew it.

If I were wise and good and rich and strong—
Fond, impious thought, if I were Walter Long—
If I could water sell like molten gold,
And make grown people do as they are told,
If over private fields and wastes as wide
As a Greek city for which heroes died,
I owned the houses and the men inside—
If all this hung on one thin thread of habit
I would not revolutionize a rabbit.

I would sit tight with all my gifts and glories,
And even preach to unconverted Tories,
That the fixed system that our land inherits,
Viewed from a certain standpoint, has its merits.

I'd guard the laws like any Radical,
And keep each precedent, however small,
However subtle, misty, dusty, dreamy,
Lest man by chance should look at me and see me;
Lest men should ask what madman made me lord
Of English ploughshares and the English sword;
Lest men should mark how sleepy is the nod
That drills the dreadful images of God!

Walter, be wise! avoid the wild and new,
The Constitution is the game for you.
Walter, beware! scorn not the gathering throng
It suffers, yet it may not suffer wrong,
It suffers, yet it cannot suffer Long.
And if you goad it these grey rules to break,
For a few pence, see that you do not wake
Death and the splendour of the scarlet cap,
Boston and Valmy, Yorktown and Jemmappes,
Freedom in arms, the riding and the routing,
The thunder of the captains and the shouting,
All that lost riot that you did not share—And
when that riot comes—you *will* be there.

THE SHAKESPEARE MEMORIAL

Lord Lilac thought it rather rotten
That Shakespeare should be quite
And therefore got on a Committee
With several chaps out of the city.
And Shorter and Sir Herbert Tree,
Lord Rothschild and Lord Rosebery
And F.C.G. and Comyns Carr,
Two dukes and a dramatic star,
Also a clergyman now dead;
And while the vain world careless sped
Unheeding the heroic name—
The souls most fed with Shakespeare's flame
Still sat unconquered in a ring,
Remembering him like anything.

Lord Lilac did not long remain.
Lord Lilac did not come again.
He softly lit a cigarette

And sought some other social set
Where, in some other knots or rings,
People were doing cultured things,
—Miss Zwilt's Humane Vivarium
—The little men that paint on gum
—The exquisite Gorilla Girl....
He sometimes, in this giddy whirl
(Not being really bad at heart),
Remembered Shakespeare with a start—
But not with that grand constancy
Of Clement Shorter, Herbert Tree,
Lord Rosebery and Comyns Carr
And all the other names there are;
Who stuck like limpets to the spot,
Lest they forgot, lest they forgot.

Lord Lilac was of slighter stuff;
Lord Lilac had had quite enough.

THE HORRIBLE HISTORY OF JONES

Jones had a dog; it had a chain;
Not often worn, not causing pain;
But, as the I.K.L. had passed
Their "Unleashed Cousins Act" at last,
Inspectors took the chain away;
Whereat the canine barked "hurray"!
At which, of course, the S.P.U.
(Whose Nervous Motorists' Bill was through),
Were forced to give the dog in charge
For being Audibly at Large.
None, you will say, were now annoyed,
Save haply Jones—the yard was void.
But something being in the lease
About "alarms to aid police,"
The U.S.U. annexed the yard
For having no sufficient guards
Now if there's one condition
The C.C.P. are strong upon
It is that every house one buys
Must have a yard for exercise;
So Jones, as tenant, was unfit.
His state of health was proof of it.

Two doctors of the T.T.U.'s
Told him his legs from long disuse,
Were atrophied; and saying "So
From step to higher step we go
Till everything is New and True,"
They cut his legs off and withdrew.
You know the E.T.S.T.'s views
Are stronger than the T.T.U.'s:
And soon (as one may say) took wing
The Arms, though not the Man, I sing.
To see him sitting limbless there
Was more than the K.K. could bear
"In mercy silence with all speed
That mouth there are no hands to feed;
What cruel sentimentalist,
O Jones, would doom thee to exist—
Clinging to selfish Selfhood yet?
Weak one! Such reasoning might upset
The Pump Act, and the accumulation
Of all constructive legislation;
Let us construct you up a bit—"
The head fell off when it was hit:
Then words did rise and honest doubt,
And four Commissions sat about
Whether the slash that left him dead
Cut off his body or his head.

An author in the Isle of Wight
Observed with unconcealed delight
A land of old and just renown
Where Freedom slowly broadened down
From Precedent to Precedent....
And this, I think, was what he meant.

THE NEW FREETHINKER

John Grubby, who was short and stout
And troubled with religious doubt,
Refused about the age of three
To sit upon the curate's knee;
(For so the eternal strife must rage
Between the spirit of the age
And Dogma, which, as is well known.

Does simply hate to be outgrown).
Grubby, the young idea that shoots,
Outgrew the ages like old boots;
While still, to all appearance, small,
Would have no Miracles at all;
And just before the age of ten
Firmly refused Free Will to men.
The altars reeled, the hen-ens shook,
Just as he read of in the book;
Flung from his house went forth the youth
Alone with tempests and the Truth,
Up to the distant city and dim
Where his papa had bought for him
A partnership in Chepe and Deer
Worth, say, twelve hundred pounds a year.
But he was resolute. Lord Brute
Had found him useful; and Lord Loot,
With whom few other men would act,
Valued his promptitude and tact;
Never did even philanthropy
Enrich a man more rapidly:
Twas he that stopped the Strike in Coal,
For hungry children racked his soul;
To end their misery there and then
He filled the mines with Chinamen—
Sat in that House that broke the Kings,
And voted for all sores of things—
And rose from Under-Sec. to Sec.
Some grumbled. Growlers who gave less
Than generous worship to success,
The little printers in Dundee
Who got ten years for blasphemy,
(Although he let them off with seven)
Respect him rather less than heaven.
No matter. This can still be said:
Never to supernatural dread,
Never to unseen deity,
Did Sir John Grubby bend the knee;
Never did dream of hell or wrath
Turn Viscount Grubby from his path;
Nor was he bribed by fabled bliss
To kneel to any world but this.
The curate lives in Camden Town,
His lap still empty of renown,
And still across the waste of years

John Grubby, in the House of Peers,
Faces that curate, proud and free,
And never sits upon his knee.

IN MEMORIAM P.D.

NICE, JANUARY 30, 1914.

If any in an island cradle curled
Of comfort, may make offerings to you,
Who in the day of all denial blew
A bugle through the blackness of the world,

An English hand would touch your shroud, in trust
That truth again be told in English speech.
And we too yet may practise what we preach,
Though it were practising the bayonet thrust.

Cutting that giant neck from sand to sand,
From sea to sea; it was a little thing
Beside your sudden shout and sabre-swing
That cut the throat of thieves in every land.

Heed not if half-wits mock your broken blade:
Mammon our master doeth all things ill.
You are the Fool that charged a windmill. Still,
The Miller is a Knave; and was afraid.

Lay down your sword. Ruin will know her own.
Let each small statesman sow his weak wild oat,
Or turn his coat to decorate his coat,
Or take the throne and perish by the throne.

Lay down your sword. And let the White Flag fade
To grey; and let the Red Flag fade to pink,
For these that climb and climb; and cannot sink
So deep as death and honour, Déroulède.

Poems

SONNET WITH THE COMPLIMENTS OF THE SEASON

TO A POPULAR LEADER MUCH TO BE CONGRATULATED ON THE AVOIDANCE OF A STRIKE AT CHRISTMAS.

I know you. You will hail the huge release,
Saying the sheathing of a thousand swords,
In silence and injustice, well accords
With Christmas bells. And you will gild with grease
The papers, the employers, the police,
And vomit up the void your windy words
To your New Christ; who bears no whip of cords
For them that traffic in the doves of peace.

The feast of friends, the candle-fruited tree,
I have not failed to honour. And I say
It would be better for such men as we,
And we be nearer Bethlehem, it we lay
Shot dead on scarlet snows for liberty,
Dead in the daylight upon Christmas Day.

A SONG OF SWORDS

"A DROVE OF CATTLE CAME INTO A VILLAGE CALLED SWORDS, AND WAS STOPPED BY THE RIOTERS."—-*Daily Paper*.

In the place called Swords on the Irish road
It is told for a new renown
How we field the horns of the cattle, and how
We will hold the horns of the devil now
Ere the lord of bell, with the horn on his brow,
Is crowned in Dublin town

Light in the East and light in the West,
And light on the cruel lords,
On the souls that suddenly all men knew,
And the green flag flew and the red flag flew,
And many a wheel of the world stopped, too,
When the cattle were stopped at Swords.

Be they sinners or less than saints

That smite in the street for rage,
We know where the shame shines bright; we know
You that they smite at, you their foe,
Lords of the lawless wage and low.
This is your lawful wage.

You pinched a child to a torture price
That you dared not name in words;
So black a jest was the silver bit
That your own speech shook for the shame of
And the coward was plain as a cow they hit
When the cattle have strayed at Swords.

The wheel of the torment of wives went round
To break men's brotherhood;
You gave the good Irish blood to grease
The clubs of your country's enemies;
You saw the brave man beat to the knees:
And you saw that it was good.

The rope of the rich is long and long—
The longest of hangmen's cords;
But the kings and crowds are holding their bream,
In a giant shadow o'er all beneath
Where God stands holding the scales of Death
Between the cattle and Swords.

Haply the lords that hire and lend,
The lowest of all men's lords,
Who sell their kind like kine at a fair.
Will find no head of their cattle there;
But faces of men where cattle were:
Faces of men—and Swords.

And the name shining and terrible,
The sternest of all man's words,
Still mark that place to seek or shun,
In the streets where the struggling cattle run—
Grass and a silence of judgment done
In the place that is called Swords.

A SONG OF DEFEAT

The line breaks and the guns go under,
The lords and the lackeys ride the plain;
I draw deep breaths of the dawn and thunder,
And the whole of my heart grows young again.
For our Chiefs said "Done," and I did not deem it;
Our Seers said "Peace," and it was not peace;
Earth will grow worse till men redeem it,
And wars more evil, ere all wars cease.
But the old flags reel and the old drums rattle.
As once in my life they throbbed and reeled;
I have found ray youth in the lost battle,
I have found my heart on the battlefield.
For we that fight till the world is free,
We are not easy in victory:
We have known each other too long, my brother,
And fought each other, the world and we.

And I dream of the days when work was scrappy,
And rare in our pockets the mark of the mint,
When we were angry and poor and happy,
And proud of seeing our names in print.
For so they conquered and so we scattered,
When the Devil rode and his dogs smelt gold,
And the peace of a harmless folk was shattered;
When I was twenty and odd years old.
When the mongrel men that the market classes
Had slimy hands upon England's rod,
And sword in hand upon Afric's passes
Her last Republic cried to God.
For the men no lords can buy or sell,
They sit not easy when all goes well.
They have said to each other what naught can smother,
They have seen each other, our souls and hell.

It is all as of old; the empty clangour.
The Nothing scrawled on a five-foot page,
The huckster who, mocking holy anger,
Painfully paints his face with rage.
And the faith of the poor is faint and partial,
And the pride of the rich is all for sale,
And the chosen heralds of England's Marshal
Are the sandwich-men of the "Daily Mail."

And the niggards that dare not give are glutted,
And the feeble that dare not fail are strong,
So while the City of Toil is gutted,
I sit in the saddle and sing my song.
For we that fight till the world is free,
We have no comfort in victory;
We have read each other as Cain his brother,
We know each other, these slaves and we.

SONNET

ON HEARING A LANDLORD ACCUSED (FALSELY, FOR ALL THE BARD CAN SAY) OF NEGLECTING ONE OF THE NUMEROUS WHITE HORSES THAT WERE OR WERE NOT CONNECTED WITH ALFRED THE GREAT

If you have picked your lawn of leaves and snails,
If you have told your valet, even with oaths,
Once a week or so, to brush your clothes.
If you have dared to clean your teeth, or nails,
While the Horse upon the holy mountain fails—
Then God that Alfred to his earth betrothes
Send on you screaming all that honour loathes,
Horsewhipping, Hounsditch, debts, and *Daily Mails*.

Can you not even conserve? For if indeed
The White Horse fades; then closer creeps the fight
When we shall scour the face of England white,
Plucking such men as you up like a weed,
And fling them far beyond a shaft shot right
When Wessex went to battle for the creed.

AFRICA

A sleepy people, without priests or kings,
Dreamed here, men say, to drive us to the sea:
O let us drive ourselves! For it is free
And smells of honour and of English things.
How came we brawling by these bitter springs,
We of the North?—two kindly nations—we?
Though the dice rattles and the clear coin rings,

Here is no place for living men to be.
Leave them the gold that worked and whined for it,
Let them that have no nation anywhere
Be native here, and fat and full of bread;
But we, whose sins were human, we will quit
The land of blood, and leave these vultures there,
Noiselessly happy, feeding on the dead.

THE DEAD HERO

We never saw you, like our sires,
For whom your face was Freedom's face,
Nor know what office-tapes and wires
With such strong cords may interlace;
We know not if the statesmen then
Were fashioned as the sort we see,
We know that not under your ken
Did England laugh at Liberty.

Yea, this one thing is known of you,
We know that not till you were dumb,
Not till your course was thundered through,
Did Mammon see his kingdom come.
The songs of theft, the swords of hire,
The clerks that raved, the troops that ran
The empire of the world's desire,
The dance of all the dirt began.

The happy jewelled alien men
Worked then but as a little leaven;
From some more modest palace then
The Soul of Dives stank to Heaven.
But when they planned with lisp and leer
Their careful war upon the weak,
They smote your body on its bier,
For surety that you could not speak.

A hero in the desert died;
Men cried that saints should bury him.
And round the grave should guard and ride,
A chivalry of Cherubim.
God said: "There is a better place,
A nobler trophy and more tall;

The beasts that fled before his face
Shall come to make his funeral.

"The mighty vermin of the void
That hid them from his bended bow,
Shall crawl from caverns overjoyed,
Jackal and snake and carrion crow.
And perched above the vulture's eggs,
Reversed upon its hideous head,
A blue-faced ape shall wave its legs
To tell the world that he is dead."

AN ELECTION ECHO 1906

This is their trumpet ripe and rounded,
They have burnt the wheat and gathered the chaff,
And we that have fought them, we that have watched them,
Have we at least not cause to laugh?

Never so low at least we stumbled—
Dead we have been but not so dead
As these that live on the life they squandered,
As these that drink of the blood they shed.

We never boasted the thing we blundered,
We never Haunted the thing that fails,
We never quailed from the living laughter,
To howl to the dead who tell no tales,

'Twas another finger at least that pointed
Our wasted men or our emptied bags,
It was not we that sounded the trumpet
In front of the triumph of wrecks and rags.

Fear not these, they have made their bargain,
They have counted the cost of the last of raids,
They have staked their lives on the things that live not,
They have burnt their house for a fire that fades.

Five years ago and we might have feared them,
Been drubbed by the coward and taught by the dunce;
Truth may endure and be told and re-echoed,
But a lie can never be young but once.

Five years ago and we might have feared them;
Now, when they lift the laurelled brow,
There shall naught go up from our hosts assembled
But a laugh like thunder. We know them now.

THE SONG OF THE WHEELS

WRITTEN DURING A FRIDAY AND SATURDAY IN AUGUST 1911.

King Dives he was waiting in his garden all alone,
Where his flowers are made of iron and his trees are made of stone,
And his hives are full of thunder and the lightning leaps and kills,
For the mills of God grind slowly; and he works with other mills.
Dives found a mighty silence; and he missed the throb and leap,
The noise of all the sleepless creatures singing him to sleep.
And he said: "A screw has fallen—or a bolt has slipped aside—
Some little thing has shifted": and the little things replied:

"Call upon the wheels, master, call upon the wheels;
We are taking rest, master, finding how it feels,
Strict the law of thine and mine: theft we ever shun—
All the wheels are thine, master—tell the wheels to run!
Yea, the Wheels are mighty gods—set them going then!
We are only men, master, have you heard of men?

"O, they live on earth like fishes, and a gasp is all their breath.
God for empty honours only gave them death and scorn of death,
And you walk the worms for carpet and you tread a stone that squeals—
Only, God that made them worms did not make them wheels.
Man shall shut his heart against you and you shall not find the spring.
Man who wills the thing he wants not, the intolerable thing—
Once he likes his empty belly better than your empty head
Earth and heaven are dumb before him: he is stronger than the dead.

"Call upon the wheels, master, call upon the wheels,
Steel is beneath your hand, stone beneath your heels,
Steel will never laugh aloud, hearing what we heard,
Stone will never break its heart, mad with hope deferred—
Men of tact that arbitrate, slow reform that heals—
Save the stinking grease, master, save it for the wheels.

"King Dives in the garden, we have naught to give or hold—
(Even while the baby came alive the rotten sticks were sold.)
The savage knows a cavern and the peasants keep a plot,
Of all the things that men have had—lo! we have them not.
Not a scrap of earth where ants could lay their eggs—
Only this poor lump of earth that walks about on legs—
Only this poor wandering mansion, only these two walking trees.
Only hands and hearts and stomachs—what have you to do with these?
You have engines big and burnished, tall beyond our fathers' ken,
Why should you make peace and traffic with such feeble folk as men?

"Call upon the wheels, master, call upon the wheels,
They are deaf to demagogues, deaf to crude appeals;
Are our hands our own, master?—how the doctors doubt!
Are our legs our own, master? wheels can run without—
Prove the points are delicate—they will understand.
All the wheels are loyal; see how still they stand!"

King Dives he was walking in his garden in the sun,
He shook his hand at heaven, and he called the wheels to run,
And the eyes of him were hateful eyes, the lips of him were curled,
And he called upon his father that is lord below the world,
Sitting in the Gate of Treason, in the gate of broken seals,
"Bend and bind them, bend and bind them, bend and bind them into wheels,
Then once more in all my garden there may swing and sound and sweep—
The noise of all the sleepless things that sing the soul to sleep."

Call upon the wheels, master, call upon the wheels.
Weary grow the holidays when you miss the meals,
Through the Gate of Treason, through the gate within,
Cometh fear and greed of fame, cometh deadly sin;
If a man grow faint, master, take him ere he kneels.
Take him, break him, rend him, end him, roll him, crush him with the wheels.

THE SECRET PEOPLE

Smile at us, pay us, pass us; but do not quite forget.
For we are the people of England, that never has spoken yet.
There is many a fat farmer that drinks less cheerfully,

There is many a free French peasant who is richer and sadder than we.
There are no folk in the whole world so helpless or so wise.
There is hunger in our bellies, there is laughter in our eyes;
You laugh at us and love us, both mugs and eyes are wet:
Only you do not know us. For we have not spoken yet.

The fine French kings came over in a flutter of flags and dames.
We liked their smiles and battles, but we never could say their names.
The blood ran red to Bosworth and the High French lords went down;
There was naught but a naked people under a naked crown.

And the eyes of the King's Servants turned terribly every way,
And the gold of the King's Servants rose higher every day.
They burnt the homes of the shaven men, that had been quaint and kind,
Till there was no bed in a monk's house, nor food that man could find.
The inns of God where no man paid, that were the wall of the weak,
The King's Servants ate them all. And Still we did not speak.

And the face of the King's Servants grew greater than the King:
He tricked them, and they trapped him, and stood round him in a ring.
The new grave lords closed round him, that had eaten the abbey's fruits.
And the men of the new religion, with their bibles in their boots.
We saw their shoulders moving, to menace or discuss,
And some were pure and some were vile; but none took heed of us.
We saw the King as they killed him, and his face was proud and pale;
And a few men talked of freedom, while England talked of ale.

A war that we understood not came over the world and woke
Americans, Frenchmen, Irish; but we knew not the things they spoke.
They talked about rights and nature and peace and the people's reign:
And the squires, our masters, bade us fight; and never scorned us again.
Weak if we be for ever, could none condemn us then;
Men called us serfs and drudges; men knew that we were men.
In foam and flame at Trafalgar, on Albuera plains,
We did and died like lions, to keep ourselves in chains,
We lay in living ruins; firing and fearing not
The strange fierce face of the Frenchmen who knew for what they fought,
And the man who seemed to be more than man we strained against and broke;
And we broke our own rights with him. And still we never spoke.

Our patch of glory ended; we never heard guns again.
But the squire seemed struck in the saddle; he was foolish, as if in pain

He leaned on a staggering lawyer, he clutched a cringing Jew,
He was stricken; it may be, after all, he was stricken at Waterloo.
Or perhaps the shades of the shaven men, whose spoil is in his house,
Come back in shining shapes at last to spoil his last carouse:
We only know the last sad squires ride slowly towards the sea.
And a new people takes the land: and still it is not we.

They have given us into the hand of the new unhappy lords,
Lords without anger and honour, who dare not carry their swords.
They fight by shuffling papers; they have bright dead alien eyes;
They look at our labour and laughter as a tired man looks at flies.
And the load 01 their loveless pity is worse than the ancient wrongs,
Their doors are shut in the evening; and they know no songs.

We hear men speaking for us of new laws strong and sweet,
Yet is there no man speaketh as we speak in the street.
It may be we shall rise the last as Frenchmen rose the first,
Our wrath come after Russia's wrath and our wrath be the worst.
It may be we are meant to mark with our riot and our rest
God's scorn for all men governing. It may be beer is best.
But we are the people of England; and we have not spoken yet.
Smile at us, pay us, pass us. But do not quite forget.

VI

MISCELLANEOUS POEMS

LOST

So you have gained the golden crowns, so you have piled together
The laurels and the jewels, the pearls out of the blue,
But I will beat the bounding drum and I will fly the feather
For all the glory I have lost, the good I never knew.

I saw the light of morning pale on princely human faces,
In tales irrevocably gone, in final night enfurled,
I saw the tail of flying fights, a glimpse of burning blisses,
And laughed to think what I had lost—the wealth of all the world.

Yea, ruined in a royal game I was before my cradle;
Was ever gambler hurling gold who lost such things as I?
The purple moth that died an hour ere I was born of

That great green sunset God shall make three days after I die.

When all the lights are lost and done, when all the skies are broken,
Above the ruin of the stars my soul shall sit in state,
With a brain made rich, with the irrevocable sunsets,
And a closed heart happy in the fullness of a fate.

So you have gained the golden crowns and grasped the golden weather,
The kingdoms and the hemispheres that all men buy and sell,
But I will lash the leaping drum and swing the flaring feather,
For the light of seven heavens that are lost to me like hell.

BALLAD OF THE SUN

O well for him that loves the sun
That sees the heaven-race ridden or run,
The splashing seas of sunset won,
And shouts for victory.

God made the sun to crown his head,
And when death's dart at last is sped,
At least it will not find him dead,
And pass the carrion by.

O ill for him that loves the sun;
Shall the sun stoop for anyone?
Shall the sun weep for hearts undone
Or heavy souls that pray?

Not less for us and everyone
Was that white web of splendour spun;
O well for him who loves the sun
Although the sun should slay.

TRANSLATION FROM DU BELLAY

Happy, who like Ulysses or that lord
Who raped the fleece, returning full and sage,
With usage and the world's wide reason stored,
With his own kin can wait the end of age.
When shall I see, when shall I see, God knows!

My little village smoke; or pass the door,
The old dear door of that unhappy house
That is to me a kingdom and much more?
Mightier to me the house my fathers made
Than your audacious heads, O Halls of Rome!
More than immortal marbles undecayed,
The thin sad slates that cover up my home;
More than your Tiber is my Loire to me,
Than Palatine my little Lyré there;
And more than all the winds of all the sea
The quiet kindness of the Angevin air.

THE HIGHER UNITY

"The Rev. Isaiah Bunter has disappeared into the interior
of the Solomon Islands, and it is feared that he may have
been devoured by the natives, as there has been a considerable
revival of religious customs among the Polynesians."
A real paragraph from a real Paper; only the names altered.

It was Isaiah Bunter
Who sailed to the world's end,
And spread religion in a way
That he did not intend.

He gave, if not the gospel-feast,
At least a ritual meal;
And in a highly painful sense
He was devoured with zeal.

And who are we (as Henson says)
That we should close the door?
And should not Evangelicals
All jump at shedding Gore?

And many a man will melt in man,
Becoming one, not two,
When smacks across the startled earth
The Kiss of Kikuyu.

When Man is the Turk, and the Atheist,
Essene, Erastian Whig,
And the Thug and the Druse and the Catholic,

And the crew of the Captain's gig.

THE EARTH'S VIGIL

The old earth keepeth her watch the same.
Alone in a voiceless void doth stand,
Her orange flowers in her bosom flame,
Her gold ring in her hand.
The surfs of the long gold-crested morns
Break ever more at her great robe's hem,
And evermore come the bleak moon-horns.
But she keepeth not watch for them.

She keepeth her watch through the awns,
But the heart of her groweth not old,
For the peal of the bridegroom's paeans,
And the tale she once was told.

The nations shock and the cities reel,
The empires travail and rive and rend,
And she looks on havoc and smoke and steel,
And knoweth it is not the end.
The faiths may choke and the powers despair,
The powers re-arise and the faiths renew,
She is only a maiden, waiting there,
For the love whose word is true.

She keepeth her watch through the aeons,
But the heart of her groweth not old,
For the peal of the bridegroom's paeans,
And the tale she once was told.

Through the cornfield's gleam and the cottage shade,
They wait unwearied, the young and old,
Mother for child and man for maid.
For a love that once was told.
The hair grows grey under thatch or slates,
The eyes grow dim behind lattice panes,
The earth-race wait as the old earth waits,
And the hope in the heart remains.

She keepeth her watch through the aeons,
But the heart of her groweth not old,

For the peal of the bridegroom's paeans,
And the tale she once was told.

God's gold ring on her hand is bound,
She fires with blossom the grey hill-sides,
Her fields are quickened, her forests crowned,
While the love of her heart abides,
And we from the fears that fret and mar
Look up in hours and behold awhile
Her face, colossal, mid star on star,
Still looking forth with a smile.

She keepeth her watch through the sons,
But the heart of her groweth not old,
For the peal of the bridegroom's paeans,
And the tale she once was told.

ON RIGHTEOUS INDIGNATION

When Adam went from Paradise
He saw the Sword and ran;
The dreadful shape, the new device,
The pointed end of Paradise,
And saw what Peril is and Price,
And knew he was a man.

When Adam went from Paradise,
He turned him back and cried
For a little flower from Paradise;
There came no flower from Paradise;
The woods were dark in Paradise,
And not a bird replied.

For only comfort or contempt,
For jest or great reward,
Over the walls of Paradise,
The flameless gates of Paradise,
The dumb shut doors of Paradise,
God flung the flaming sword.

It burns the hand that holds it
More than the skull it scores;
It doubles like a snake and stings,

Yet he in whose hand it swings
He is the most masterful of things,
A scorner of the stars.

WHEN I CAME BACK TO FLEET STREET

When I came back to Fleet Street,
Through a sunset nook at night,
And saw the old Green Dragon
With the windows all alight,
And hailed the old Green Dragon
And the Cock I used to know,
Where all good fellows were my friends
A little while ago;

I had been long in meadows,
And the trees took hold of me,
And the still towns in the beech-woods,
Where men were meant to be.
But old things held; the laughter,
The long unnatural night,
And all the truth they talk in hell,
And all the lies they write.

For I came back to Fleet Street,
And not in peace I came;
A cloven pride was in my heart,
And half my love was shame.
I came to fight in fairy-tale,
Whose end shall no man know—
To fight the old Green Dragon
Until the Cock shall crow!

Under the broad bright windows
Of men I serve no more,
The groaning of the old great wheels
Thickened to a throttled roar;
All buried things broke upward;
And peered from its retreat,
Ugly and silent, like an elf,
The secret of the street.

They did not break the padlocks,

Or clear the wall away.
The men in debt that drank of old
Still drink in debt to-day;
Chained to the rich by ruin,
Cheerful in chains, as then
When old unbroken Pickwick walked
Among the broken men.

Still he that dreams and rambles
Through his own elfin air,
Knows that the street's a prison,
Knows that the gates are there:
Still he that scorns or struggles
Sees, frightful and afar.
All that they leave of rebels
Rot high on Temple Bar.

All that I loved and hated,
All that I shunned and knew,
Clears in broad battle lightning,
Where they, and I, and you,
Run high the barricade that breaks
The barriers of the street,
And shout to them that shrink within,
The Prisoners of the Fleet.

A CIDER SONG

To J.S.M.

EXTRACT FROM A ROMANCE WHICH IS NOT YET
WRITTEN AND PROBABLY NEVER WILL BE.

The wine they drink in Paradise
They make in Haute Lorraine;
God brought it burning from the sod
To be a sign and signal rod
That they that drink the blood of God
Shall never thirst again.

The wine they praise in Paradise
They make in Ponterey,
The purple wine of Paradise,

But we have better at the price;
It's wine they praise in Paradise,
It's cider that they pray.

The wine they want in Paradise
They find in Plodder's End,
The apple wine of Hereford,
Of Hafod Hill and Hereford,
Where woods went down to Hereford,
And there I had a friend.

The soft feet of the blessed go
In the soft western vales,
The road the silent saints accord,
The road from Heaven to Hereford,
Where the apple wood of Hereford
Goes all the way to Wales.

THE LAST HERO

The wind blew out from Bergen from the dawning to the day,
There was a wreck of trees and fall of towers a score of miles away,
And drifted like a livid leaf I go before its tide,
Spewed out of house and stable, beggared of flag and bride.
The heavens are bowed about my head, shouting like seraph wars.
With rains that might put out the sun and clean the sky of stars,
Rains like the fall of ruined seas from secret worlds above,
The roaring of the rains of God none but the lonely love.
Feast in my hall, O foemen, and eat and drink and drain,
You never loved the sun in heaven as I have loved the rain.

The chance of battle changes—so may all battle be;
I stole my lady bride from them, they stole her back from me.
I rent her from her red-roofed hall, I rode and saw arise
More lovely than the living flowers the hatred in her eyes.
She never loved me, never bent, never was less divine;
The sunset never loved me; the wind was never mine.
Was it all nothing that she stood imperial in duresse?
Silence itself made softer with the sweeping of her dress.
O you who drain the cup of life, O you who wear the crown,
You never loved a woman's smile as I have loved her frown.

The wind blew out from Bergen from the dawning to the day,

They ride and run with fifty spears to break and bar my way,
I shall not die alone, alone, but kin to all the powers.
As merry as the ancient sun and fighting like the flowers.
How white their steel, how bright their eyes! I love each laughing knave.
Cry high and bid him welcome to the banquet of the brave.
Yea, I will bless them as they bend and love them where they lie,
When on their skulls the sword I swing falls shattering from the sky.
The hour when death is like a light and blood is like a rose,—
You never loved your friends, my friends, as I shall love my foes.

Know you what earth shall lose to-night, what rich, uncounted loans,
What heavy gold of tales untold you bury with my bones?
My loves in deep dim meadows, my ships that rode at ease,
Ruffling the purple plumage of strange and secret seas.
To see this fair earth as it is to me alone was given,
The blow that breaks my brow to-night shall break the dome of heaven.
The skies I saw, the trees I saw after no eyes shall see.
To-night I die the death of God; the stars shall die with me:
One sound shall sunder all the spears and break the trumpet's breath:
You never laughed in all your life as I shall laugh in death.

VII

BALLADES

BALLADE D'UNE GRANDE DAME

Heaven shall forgive you Bridge at dawn,
The clothes you wear—or do not wear—
And Ladies' Leap-frog on the lawn
And dyes and drugs, and *petits verres.*
Your vicious things shall melt in air ...
... But for the Virtuous Things you do,
The Righteous Work, the Public Care,
It shall not be forgiven you.

Because you could not even yawn
When your Committees would prepare
To have the teeth of paupers drawn,
Or strip the slums of Human Hair;
Because a Doctor Otto Maehr

Spoke of "a segregated few"—
And you sat smiling in your chair—
It shall not be forgiven you.

Though your sins cried to—-Father Vaughan,
These desperate you could not spare
Who steal, with nothing left to pawn;
You caged a man up like a bear
For ever in a jailor's care
Because his sins were more than *two* ...
... I know a house in Hoxton where
It shall not be forgiven you.

ENVOI

Princess, you trapped a guileless Mayor
To meet some people that you knew ...
When the Last Trumpet rends the air
It shall not be forgiven you.

A BALLADE OF AN ANTI-PURITAN

They spoke of Progress spiring round,
Of Light and Mrs. Humphry Ward—
It is not true to say I frowned,
Or ran about the room and roared;
I might have simply sat and snored—
I rose politely in the club
And said, "I feel a little bored;
Will someone take me to a pub?"

The new world's wisest did surround
Me; and it pains me to record
I did not think their views profound,
Or their conclusions well assured;
The simple life I can't afford,
Besides, I do not like the grub—
I wait a mash and sausage, "scored"—
Will someone take me to a pub?

I know where Men can still be found,
Anger and clamorous accord,
And virtues growing from the ground,

And fellowship of beer and board,
And song, that is a sturdy cord.
And hope, that is a hardy shrub,
And goodness, that is God's last word—
Will someone take me to a pub?

ENVOI

Prince, Bayard would have smashed his sword
To see the sort of knights you dub—Is
that the last of them—O Lord!
Will someone take me to a pub?

A BALLADE OF A BOOK-REVIEWER

I have not read a rotten page
Of "Sex-Hate" or "The Social Test,"
And here comes "Husks" and "Heritage"....
O Moses, give us all a rest!
"Ethics of Empire"!... I protest
I will not even cut the strings,
I'll read "Jack Redskin on the Quest"
And feed my brain with better things.

Somebody wants a Wiser Age
(He also wants me to invest);
Somebody likes the Finnish Stage
Because the Jesters do not jest;
And grey with dust is Dante's crest,
The bell of Rabelais soundless swings;
And the winds come out of the west
And feed my brain with better things.

Lord of our laughter and our rage.
Look on us with our sins oppressed!
I, too, have trodden mine heritage,
Wickedly wearying of the best.
Burn from my brain and from my breast
Sloth, and the cowardice that clings,
And stiffness and the soul's arrest:
And feed my brain with better things.

ENVOI

Prince, you are host and I am guest,
Therefore I shrink from cavillings....
But I should have that fizz suppressed
And feed my brain with better things.

A BALLADE OF SUICIDE

The gallows in my garden, people say,
Is new and neat and adequately tall.
I tie the noose on in a knowing way
As one that knots his necktie for a ball;
But just as all the neighbours—on the wall—
Are drawing a long breath to shout "Hurray!"
The strangest whim has seized me.... After all
I think I will not hang myself to-day.

To-morrow is the time I get my pay—My
uncle's sword is hanging in the hall—
I see a little cloud all pink and grey—
Perhaps the rector's mother will *not* call—
I fancy that I heard from Mr. Gall
That mushrooms could be cooked another way—
I never read the works of Juvenal—
I think I will not hang myself to-day.

The world will have another washing day;
The decadents decay; the pedants pall;
And H.G. Wells has found that children play.
And Bernard Shaw discovered that they squall;
Rationalists are growing rational—
And through thick woods one finds a stream astray,
So secret that the very sky seems small—
I think I will not hang myself to-day.

ENVOI

Prince, I can hear the trumpet of Germinal,
The tumbrils toiling up the terrible way;
Even to-day your royal head may fall—
I think I will not hang myself to-day.

A BALLADE OF THE FIRST RAIN

The sky is blue with summer and the sun,
The woods are brown as autumn with the tan,
It might as well be Tropics and be done,
I might as well be born a copper Khan;
I fashion me an oriental fan
Made of the wholly unreceipted bills
Brought by the ice-man, sleeping in his van
(A storm is coming on the Chiltern Hills).

I read the Young Philosophers for fun
—Fresh as our sorrow for the late Queen Anne—
The Dionysians whom a pint would stun,
The Pantheists who never heard of Pan.
—But through my hair electric needles ran,
And on my book a gout of water spills,
And on the skirts of heaven the guns began
(A storm is coming on the Chiltern Hills).

O fields of England, cracked and dry and dun,
O soul of England, sick of words, and wan!—
The clouds grow dark;—the down-rush has begun.
—It comes, it comes, as holy darkness can,
Black as with banners, ban and arriere-ban;
A falling laughter all the valley fills,
Deep as God's thunder and the thirst of man:
(A storm is coming on the Chiltern Hills).

ENVOI

Prince, Prince-Elective on the modern plan
Fulfilling such a lot of People's Wills,
You take the Chiltern Hundreds while you can—
A storm is coming on the Chiltern Hills.

www.ingramcontent.com/pod-product-compliance
Lightning Source LLC
Chambersburg PA
CBHW030456010526
44118CB00011B/969